ROBERT IRVINE

ROBERT IRVINE

With more than 25 years in the culinary profession, there aren't many places Chef Robert Irvine hasn't cooked or challenges he hasn't had to cook his way out of. During his time in the British Royal Navy and in the years that followed, Robert has cooked his way through Europe, the Far East, the Caribbean and the Americas, in hotels, on the high seas and even for the Academy Awards.

As the host of one of the Food Network's highest rated shows, Restaurant: Impossible, Robert is best known for saving struggling restaurants across America by assessing and overhauling the restaurant's weakest spots.

Robert is the author of two cookbooks, "Mission: Cook!" and "Impossible to Easy" and lifestyle book, "Fit Fuel".

I would like to thank everyone that made this book possible. First to my family, my wife Gail and my daughters Annalise and Talia. A very special thank you to Cat Chancey, my food stylist, for her endless hours of testing recipes and then bringing it all together so this cookbook is just right for you, the HSN customer. Also to photographer and editor Daniel Koren, food stylists Judy Ayers and Jen Stewart, as well as everyone at Celebrity Cookware - Syd, Arnie, Mike, Phoebe, Nicolle, Michael and the rest of the staff.

Robert Irvine

TABLE OF CONTENTS

BLEND ANYTHING MACHINE

CHOPPER BOWL WITH CHOPPER BLADES

The Chopper Bowl with Chopper Blades has many remarkable uses for making your favorite appetizer, lunch, dinner and even desserts. The bowl has a 50-ounce capacity which makes it larger than small food processors, yet it is small enough to keep handy on your kitchen counter for everyday use.

Using fresh ingredients whenever possible is essential to successful cooking and the Chopper Bowl will allow you to chop garlic, onions, celery, carrots and many other vegetables quickly and efficiently.

Some fruits and vegetables can go in whole, while some need to be cut first prior to placing them into the Chopper Bowl to ensure even processing. Firm vegetables like carrots should be cut into 1/2-inch pieces while softer vegetables like onions should be cut into 1 1/2-inch pieces before processing.

Use Speed Selector Button 1 for softer foods and Speed Selector Button 2 for harder foods.

Do not operate the motor continuously for more than 30 seconds when using the chopper attachment to prevent food from being too finely chopped. You can also pulse using either Speed Selector Button to achieve your desired consistency.

Some foods require you to scrape down the sides of the Chopper Bowl periodically during processing using a rubber spatula to allow the blades to reach all the ingredients. Also remember to not overfill the Chopper Bowl with ingredients to allow the blades to function properly.

USING A SINGLE CHOPPER BLADE

If processing a small amount of ingredients, or if chopping softer foods you think might get over processed, you can use the Chopper Bowl with just a single blade instead of the dual blades. Just use the lower Chopper Blade and leave the upper Chopper Blade out.

BLENDING ROD

The Blending Rod is fantastic for making a variety of things from healthy fresh salad dressings and soups to indulgent milkshakes and hot chocolate. You can blend your dressings and mayonnaise in the same container you will store them in which will speed up the cleaning process as there are no additional containers to be cleaned.

USING THE BLENDING ROD IN HOT LIQUIDS

Always use care when immersing the Blending Rod in hot liquids such as soups. To avoid splashing, always insert the Blending Rod into the bottom of the liquid first and begin pureeing using Speed Selector Button 1 then increase speed if needed. Always make sure the motor is not running when lifting the rod out of the hot liquid to prevent injury from hot liquid splatter. An excellent benefit of using the Blending Rod is that you can blend directly in the stockpot or other cooking vessel you're already using. No need to transfer the liquids to a separate bowl or container just to blend.

USING THE BLENDING ROD IN TALL CONTAINERS OR CANNING JARS

Using a tall container or jar with the Blending Rod will ensure better blending because it helps blend more ingredients at once. When making mayonnaise, aioli or dressings, always begin with the Blending Rod inserted into the bottom of the container then begin moving up and down until all of the ingredients are emulsified. If using to make a smoothie containing frozen fruit, begin at the top of the ingredients and press down on the ingredients until you reach the bottom, then move up and down until all the ingredients are pureed to your desired consistency.

CHOPPER BOWL WITH EMULSIFYING DISC

This disc is used to aerate ingredients and will amaze you the very first time you make a fat-free topping for your coffee, latte or hot chocolate. Just put the Emulsifying Disc into the Chopper Bowl, add enough skim milk to cover the flat part of the disc and enjoy creamy froth within seconds. Also use it to make dressings, beat egg whites for meringue or omelettes as well as to make desserts such as mousse.

CLEANING

Clean the Blending Rod, Chopper Bowl, Chopper Blades and Emulsifying Disc in warm, soapy water without harsh abrasive cleaners.

Both the Chopper Bowl Cover and Motor should only be wiped down with a damp cloth and not be immersed in water.

Using a straw cleaning brush to clean the center of the Chopper Blades is extremely helpful to reach foods that may be hard to reach and remove. A straw cleaning brush can be purchased at any home goods store and most grocery stores.

Cooking & Prep Tips

CUTTING VEGETABLES

Some ingredients need to be cut prior to chopping in the Chopper Bowl to ensure even chopping. Cut hard vegetables such as carrots, radishes, ginger and celery into 1/2-inch pieces and soft vegetables like onions and tomatoes into 1 1/2-inch pieces. If you are cutting vegetables for soup, always cut into 1/2-inch pieces as they need to be able to fit under the blade of the Blending Rod in order to puree properly.

CUTTING FRUIT

When chopping fruit in the Chopper Bowl, cut the fruit into 1/2-inch slices. Since frozen fruits are sold already sliced in the package there is no need to cut down further prior to chopping when making ice cream or sorbet. Just add the fruit, juice or milk and process.

RAW MEATS

You can use the Chopper Bowl with Chopper Blades to make your own ground meat. Most chicken breasts and fish can be put in whole providing each piece does not exceed 6 ounces in weight and 3/4-inch in thickness. When grinding steak, cut the steak into 2-inch strips or cubes.

JUICE

Using the juice from fresh lemons, limes, oranges and grapefruit is recommended over store-bought juice. The easiest method is to roll the desired whole citrus on a countertop then firmly press on the citrus to release the juices inside before cutting in half and squeezing the juice for cooking. Most grocery stores also carry inexpensive hand juicers to help make fresh juice as fast as opening a jar of concentrated juice. If you choose to buy store-bought juice check the list of ingredients to make sure you are buying 100 percent juice. Most markets will carry them in the health food section.

OIL

Grapeseed oil is used throughout this cookbook, however you can substitute your favorite oil in all of the recipes if you prefer. Grapeseed oil has a very light taste compared to other oils which allows the other fresh ingredients to flavor your food instead of the oil. It also has a relatively high smoke point which makes it excellent for sautéing.

CASTER SUGAR

Caster Sugar is a superfine sugar that has a lighter texture than granulated sugar. It is often used in this book for making frozen drinks and dessert recipes as it dissolves quickly. You can use granulated sugar cup-for-cup instead but using caster sugar will result in a smoother consistency. You can purchase it in most fine markets however it is easy to make with this wonderful appliance by following the recipe on page 51.

BUTTER

The butter used throughout the book is unsalted butter as it allows for better control of how much salt is used. The salt content of salted butter varies by brand and using unsalted butter makes for a more precise use of salt. If you use salted butter because you happen to have it on hand, reduce the salt in the recipe by approximately 1/4 teaspoon or adjust to your individual taste.

HONEY PEANUT BUTTER

=== MAKES 1 CUP ===

INGREDIENTS

8 ounces salted peanuts
3 tablespoons honey
1/4 cup peanut oil

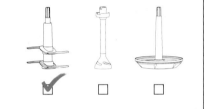

METHOD

1. Place peanuts into the Chopper Bowl fitted with the Chopper Blades.
2. Pulse using Speed Selector Button 2 until peanuts are chopped into small pieces.
3. Scrape down the sides of the Chopper Bowl using a rubber spatula then add the honey and the peanut oil so that all of the ingredients are on the bottom of the bowl.
4. Press Speed Selector Button 2 for 20 seconds then carefully scrape the mixture from the sides of the Chopper Bowl and repeat until desired consistency is achieved (this process can take up to 3 minutes).
5. Use as desired and store in an airtight container in the refrigerator for up to 3 months.

★★★★★
CHERMOULA CHICKEN

═══ MAKES 4 SERVINGS ═══

INGREDIENTS

For the Marinade:
1 cup grapeseed oil

1 1/2 cups cilantro leaves

1 1/2 cups parsley leaves

2 tablespoons ground cumin

3 garlic cloves

1 teaspoon salt

1 teaspoon black pepper

1 shallot

Zest and juice from 1 lemon

1 teaspoon chili powder

1 teaspoon Hungarian paprika

1 teaspoon turmeric powder

For the Chicken:
4 raw boneless skinless chicken breasts

1 tablespoon grapeseed oil

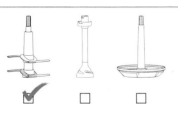

METHOD

1. Place all marinade ingredients in the order listed into the Chopper Bowl fitted with the Chopper Blades.

2. Pulse using Speed Selector Button 2 for 20 seconds.

3. Place chicken into a 1-gallon zipper bag then add 1/2 cup marinade and refrigerate for a minimum of 1 hour (this step can be done a day ahead if desired).

4. Remove chicken from refrigerator and let rest for 10 minutes.

5. Preheat the grapeseed oil in a large skillet over medium heat.

6. Add chicken to the skillet and cook on medium heat for approximately 5 minutes on each side or until internal temperature reaches 165°F on a meat thermometer.

7. Remove, garnish as desired and serve with your choice of sides.

TIP

If you don't like cilantro, you can double the amount of parsley instead of using cilantro.

★★★★★ BASIL PESTO

MAKES 2 CUPS

INGREDIENTS

2 cups packed fresh basil leaves

2 garlic cloves

1/4 cup pine nuts

2 tablespoons Parmesan cheese, grated

1/2 cup grapeseed oil

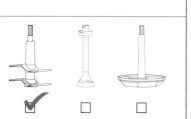

METHOD

1. Combine all ingredients in the Chopper Bowl fitted with the Chopper Blades.

2. Press Speed Selector Button 2 for 20-30 seconds or until all ingredients are combined.

3. Serve as desired on pasta, chicken as well as bread or mix it into the mayonnaise on page 78.

4. Pesto can be kept in the refrigerator for up to 2 weeks.

TIP

Remaining pesto can be frozen for up to 4 months.

★★★★★
FRESH TOMATO SALSA

MAKES 2 CUPS

INGREDIENTS

8 Campari tomatoes

1/4 white onion

1 garlic clove

1 jalapeño pepper, halved and seeds removed

10 cilantro sprigs

Juice from 1/2 lime

1 tablespoon grapeseed oil

Pinch of sea salt or kosher salt

Tortilla chips for serving

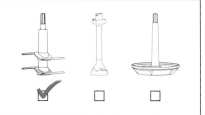

METHOD

1. Place all ingredients, except tortilla chips, into the Chopper Bowl fitted with the Chopper Blades.
2. Pulse 4-5 times using Speed Selector Button 1 or until desired consistency.
3. Serve with tortilla chips.

★ ★ ★ ★ ★
CREAMY BEET SOUP

=== **MAKES 4 SERVINGS** ===

INGREDIENTS

1 small yellow onion, cut into
1-inch pieces

3 garlic cloves

1 ginger coin

1 tablespoon grapeseed oil

3 large red beets, peeled and cut
into 1/4-inch pieces

5 cups vegetable stock, divided

1/2 teaspoon kosher salt

1/4 teaspoon black pepper

1 can (13.66 ounces) low-fat
coconut milk

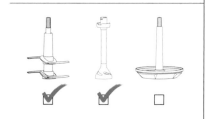

METHOD

1. Place onions, garlic and ginger into the Chopper Bowl fitted with the Chopper Blades.

2. Pulse using Speed Selector Button 2 for 20 seconds or until all ingredients are chopped but not over processed.

3. Preheat oil in a large stockpot over medium heat.

4. Sauté the onion mixture for 3 minutes while stirring often or until onions are clear.

5. Add the beets, 4 cups of stock, salt and pepper then bring to a boil.

6. Reduce the heat to simmer and cook uncovered for 20 minutes or until beets are fork tender.

7. Using the Blending Rod inserted into the bottom of the stockpot, puree with Speed Selector Button 1 for 30 seconds or until smooth. Add the coconut milk and remaining cup of vegetable stock then blend until combined (do not remove the Blending Rod from the pot while running to void splatter).

8. Garnish as desired and serve.

TIP — If you have difficulty cutting the beets while raw, you can bake them in the oven at 350°F for one hour to soften. Let cool before cutting into pieces.

★ ★ ★ ★ ★

★★★★★
No Sugar Added
Strawberry Banana
Ice Cream

MAKES 4 SERVINGS

INGREDIENTS

8 ounces frozen strawberries

1 cup sliced frozen bananas (approximately 2 bananas)

1/2 cup heavy cream (or use a non-dairy based cream or milk)

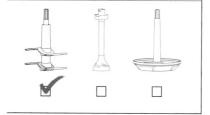

METHOD

1. Place all ingredients into the Chopper Bowl fitted with the Chopper Blades.

2. Press Speed Selector Button 2 for 20 seconds then carefully scrape down the sides of the Chopper Bowl and repeat until smooth and creamy (this process can take up to 2 1/2 minutes).

3. Serve immediately.

★ ★ ★ ★ ★

TIP

If you prefer harder ice cream, freeze in a freezer-safe container for 2-3 hours to harden.

★★★★★ FROZEN SHIRLEY TEMPLE

MAKES 1 SERVING

INGREDIENTS

2 cups ice

3 ounces lemon-lime soda

3 ounces ginger ale

1 1/2 ounces grenadine

Maraschino cherry for garnish
(optional)

METHOD

1. Place all ingredients, except cherry, in the order listed into the Chopper Bowl fitted with the Chopper Blades.
2. Press Speed Selector Button 2 for 20 seconds, pause for a few seconds then pulse using Speed Selector Button 2 until all of the ice is crushed evenly.
3. Pour into glass, garnish with a cherry if desired and serve immediately.

Cucumber & Tomato Salad

★★★★★

MAKES 4 SERVINGS

INGREDIENTS

1/4 red onion, cut into 1/2-inch pieces

1 garlic clove

1/4 cup fresh flat leaf parsley

1 tablespoon fresh dill

1/4 cup grapeseed oil

2 tablespoons pear infused vinegar

1 teaspoon Dijon mustard

1 teaspoon kosher salt

1/2 teaspoon black pepper

2 cups English cucumbers, halved lengthwise then quartered

2 cups grape tomatoes, halved

METHOD

1. Place the onion, garlic, parsley and dill into the Chopper Bowl fitted with the Chopper Blades.

2. Pulse using Speed Selector Button 2 for 5 seconds or until all the herbs and garlic are chopped.

3. Add the oil, vinegar, mustard, salt and pepper to the Chopper Bowl.

4. Press Speed Selector Button 2 for 20 seconds or until ingredients are emulsified.

5. In a large bowl combine the cucumbers, tomatoes and dressing then toss and serve.

★ ★ ★ ★ ★
Baked Fish Tacos With Mango Salsa

MAKES 2-4 SERVINGS

INGREDIENTS

For the Fish:

1/2 teaspoon dried oregano

1/2 teaspoon chili powder

1/2 teaspoon garlic powder

1/2 teaspoon coriander

1/4 teaspoon ground cumin

1/4 teaspoon kosher salt

1 pound halibut

1 tablespoon grapeseed oil

Juice from 1 lime

Corn tortillas for serving

For the Salsa:

3 whole mangos, peeled and sliced

1/2 red bell pepper, cut into 2-inch chunks

1/4 small red onion

2 tablespoons fresh cilantro (about 6 sprigs)

1/2 jalapeño pepper, seeded

Juice of 2 limes

1/8 teaspoon kosher salt

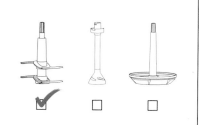

METHOD

1. Preheat oven to 375°F.

2. Combine oregano, chili powder, garlic powder, coriander, ground cumin and salt in a small bowl.

3. Brush both sides of the halibut with grapeseed oil and place in a baking dish.

4. Squeeze lime juice over the halibut then sprinkle seasoning mix over the fish and bake uncovered for 12 minutes or until internal temperature reaches 140°F on a meat thermometer.

5. While fish is baking, place all salsa ingredients into the Chopper Bowl fitted with the Chopper Blades.

6. Pulse 4-5 times using Speed Selector Button 1 or until desired consistency is achieved.

7. Serve as desired with corn tortillas.

TIP

For a lighter
variation, serve
on butter lettuce
instead of tortillas.

★★★★★
ORANGE PINEAPPLE SORBET

=== **MAKES 2 SERVINGS** ===

INGREDIENTS

8 ounces frozen pineapple

1/2 cup orange juice

2 tablespoons caster sugar
(page 51)

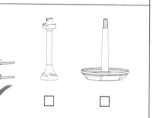

METHOD

1. Place all ingredients in the order listed into the Chopper Bowl fitted with the Chopper Blades.

2. Press Speed Selector Button 2 for 30 seconds, let pineapple chunks settle then repeat until smooth (this process can take up to 2 minutes).

3. Serve immediately.

TIP

Substitute the orange juice with heavy whipping cream to make pineapple ice cream.

★★★★★ FRESH HERB HUMMUS

=== MAKES 1 1/2 CUPS ===

INGREDIENTS

1 cup mixed herbs (dill, basil, parsley, tarragon, chives)

1 garlic clove

1 can (15 ounces) chickpeas, drained

2 tablespoons tahini

Juice and zest from 1 lemon

1/4 cup grapeseed oil

1/2 teaspoon salt

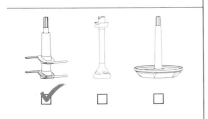

METHOD

1. Place mixed herbs and garlic into the Chopper Bowl fitted with the Chopper Blades.
2. Pulse 4-5 times using Speed Selector Button 2 or until chopped.
3. Using a rubber spatula, scrape down the herbs from the sides of the Chopper Bowl then add remaining ingredients.
4. Press Speed Selector Button 2 for 20-30 seconds until mixture is smooth.
5. Serve with fresh cut raw vegetables, chips or flatbreads for a healthy snack.

TIP — Use this to give great flavor to any sandwich in place of mayonnaise.

CHICKEN SALAD WRAP

★ ★ ★ ★ ★

MAKES 2 SERVINGS

INGREDIENTS

2 cups cooked chicken pieces (or leftover chicken)

1 celery stalk, cut into 1/2-inch pieces

2 green onions, cut into 1/2-inch pieces

1 tablespoon lemon juice

2 tablespoons mayonnaise

2 hard boiled eggs

2 tablespoons pickle relish

1 teaspoon yellow mustard

2 spinach tortillas

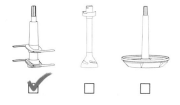

METHOD

1. Place all ingredients, except tortillas, in the order listed into the Chopper Bowl fitted with the Chopper Blades.
2. Pulse using Speed Selector Button 2 for 15-20 seconds or until desired consistency is achieved.
3. Divide the chicken salad between the tortillas then fold like a burrito and serve.

TIP

You can buy already cooked chicken from the deli at your grocery store.

22

★★★★★
CASHEW BUTTER

MAKES 1 CUP

INGREDIENTS

8 ounces unsalted cashews

2 tablespoons honey

1 teaspoon vanilla extract

2 tablespoons grapeseed oil

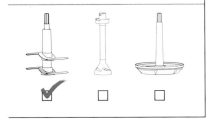

METHOD

1. Preheat oven to 350°F.
2. Place cashews on a cookie sheet or in an oven-safe dish and bake at 350°F for 6 minutes.
3. Remove from oven then transfer cashews to the Chopper Bowl fitted with the Chopper Blades.
4. Pulse using Speed Selector Button 2 until cashews are chopped into small pieces.
5. Add remaining ingredients to the Chopper Bowl.
6. Press Speed Selector Button 2 for 30 seconds then stop and carefully scrape the mixture from the sides of the Chopper Bowl. Repeat until desired consistency is achieved (this may take up to 3 minutes).
7. Remove and use as desired.

TIP

Heating the cashews shortens processing time. You can also heat the cashews in the microwave for 90 seconds.

★ ★ ★ ★ ★
SPICY 3 PEPPER HUMMUS

MAKES 2 CUPS

INGREDIENTS

2 cans (16 ounces each) chickpeas, drained

2 tablespoons grapeseed oil

Juice from 1 lemon

2 tablespoons tahini

8 garlic cloves

1 tablespoon jarred jalapeño pepper slices

1 teaspoon liquid from the jar of jalapeño peppers

1 teaspoon salt

1/2 teaspoon black pepper

1 1/2 teaspoons cayenne pepper

1/2 teaspoon ground cumin

Leaves from 2 oregano sprigs

Tortilla chips for serving

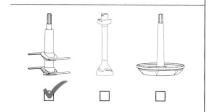

METHOD

1. Place all ingredients, except tortilla chips, in the order listed into the Chopper Bowl fitted with the Chopper Blades.

2. Press Speed Selector Button 2 for 20-30 seconds until all ingredients are smooth.

3. Garnish as desired and serve with tortilla chips.

TIP

This hummus was made with chickpeas however you can substitute the chickpeas with white beans or pinto beans to make a different variation of this recipe. This hummus also makes an excellent sandwich spread.

★★★★★ OLIVE TAPENADE

MAKES 2 CUPS

INGREDIENTS

1 cup black pitted olives

1 cup Spanish green olives

1 tablespoon capers

1/4 cup sun dried tomatoes

2 garlic cloves

2 basil leaves, torn

2 sprigs thyme, leaves only

2 sprigs parsley, torn

1/4 cup grapeseed oil

Toasted bread slices for serving

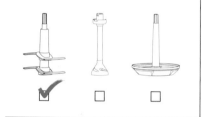

METHOD

1. Place all ingredients, except bread slices, into the Chopper Bowl fitted with a single Chopper Blade (lower Chopper Blade).

2. Pulse using Speed Selector Button 2 for 15 seconds or until desired consistency is achieved.

3. Serve on toasted bread or crackers.

TIP

Use only 1 Chopper Blade in the Chopper Bowl to avoid over processing as this recipe can quickly turn into a paste.

★★★★★
LIMEADE SLUSHY

═══ MAKES 1 SERVING ═══

INGREDIENTS

2 cups ice

2 ounces freshly squeezed
lime juice

Zest from 1/2 lime

2 ounces simple syrup

1 ounce Vodka

Mint leaf for garnish

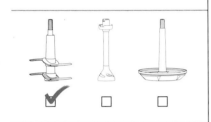

METHOD

1. Place all ingredients, except mint, in the order listed into the Chopper Bowl fitted with the Chopper Blades.

2. Press Speed Selector Button 2 for 20 seconds, pause for a few seconds then pulse using Speed Selector Button 2 until all of the ice is crushed evenly.

3. Pour into glass, garnish with mint and serve immediately.

FRESH HERB VINAIGRETTE

★ ★ ★ ★ ★

MAKES 1 CUP

INGREDIENTS

1/4 cup fresh parsley sprigs

Leaves from 2 oregano sprigs

4 basil leaves

1 garlic clove

1/2 cup grapeseed oil

1/4 cup red wine vinegar

1/2 teaspoon kosher salt

1/4 teaspoon black pepper

1 tablespoon honey

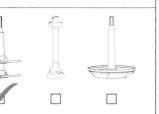

METHOD

1. Place all ingredients in the order listed into the Chopper Bowl fitted with the Chopper Blades.

2. Press Speed Selector Button 2 for 20 seconds or until all ingredients are chopped and oil and vinegar are emulsified.

3. Serve over your favorite salad, or use on cooked tortellini for a refreshing pasta salad.

TIP

This recipe uses fresh parsley, oregano and basil but you can substitute with other fresh herbs of your choice like sage, tarragon or thyme. You can also substitute the red wine vinegar with any vinegar of your choice.

★★★★★ SALMON BURGERS

MAKES 4 SERVINGS

INGREDIENTS

3 green onions, cut into 1/2-inch pieces

1 tablespoon capers, drained

1 tablespoon lemon juice

1 tablespoon tarragon

1 teaspoon Dijon mustard

1 teaspoon store-bought horseradish

1/2 cup panko

1/2 teaspoon salt

1/2 teaspoon black pepper

1 pound salmon fillets, skin removed, roughly cut into 2-inch pieces

1 tablespoon grapeseed oil

4 whole wheat buns

1 cup arugula

4 tablespoons Sriracha Aioli (page 75)

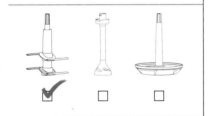

METHOD

1. Preheat a skillet over medium heat.

2. Place the green onions, capers, lemon juice, tarragon, Dijon mustard, horseradish, panko, salt and pepper into the Chopper Bowl fitted with the Chopper Blades.

3. Pulse 4-5 times using Speed Selector Button 2 or until all ingredients are chopped.

4. Add the salmon pieces then pulse using Speed Selector Button 1 for 10 seconds or until salmon pieces are coarsely chopped.

5. Remove mixture from Chopper Bowl then divide into four 1-inch thick patties.

6. Pour the grapeseed oil into the heated skillet and let heat for 1 minute.

7. Add patties to the skillet and cook for 3 minutes on each side or until nicely browned.

8. Serve on whole wheat buns topped with sriracha aioli or your favorite sandwich spread.

TIP

For a less spicy alternative, mix 3 tablespoons fresh herb hummus (page 21) with 1 tablespoon mayonnaise or greek yogurt then top on the burgers instead of using the sriracha aioli.

★★★★★ FETTUCCINI ALFREDO

MAKES 4 SERVINGS

INGREDIENTS

4 ounces Parmesan-Reggiano, cut into 1-inch cubes

1 garlic clove

2 teaspoons black pepper

1 teaspoon salt

2 cups heavy cream

16 ounces Fettuccini, cooked as directed on package

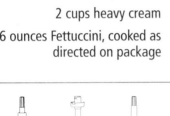

METHOD

1. Place Parmesan cubes, garlic, black pepper and salt into the Chopper Bowl fitted with the Chopper Blades.
2. Press Speed Selector Button 2 for 30 seconds or until the Parmesan is grated; set aside.
3. In a deep skillet, bring the heavy cream to a boil.
4. Add Chopper Bowl contents to the boiling heavy cream then whisk for about 2 minutes or until smooth and cheese has melted.
5. Reduce heat to a simmer and continue cooking for 5 minutes, stirring occasionally.
6. Stir the cooked Fettuccini into the sauce in the skillet using a pasta fork or tongs until covered.
7. Garnish as desired and serve immediately.

TIP

Top pasta with fresh basil, oregano or thyme for added flavor.

HAM & SWISS MINI MUFFINS

★ ★ ★ ★ ★

=== MAKES 24 MUFFINS ===

INGREDIENTS

2 1/2 ounces ham, diced into 1/2-inch cubes

1 small white onion, cut into 8 pieces

1/2 cup Swiss cheese, grated

1 whole egg

1/4 teaspoon black pepper

1 1/2 teaspoons Dijon mustard

1 package (8 ounces) store-bought crescent rolls

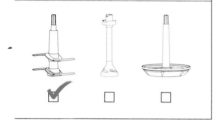

METHOD

1. Preheat oven to 350°F.
2. Apply nonstick spray to a mini muffin tin and set aside.
3. Place ham, onions, Swiss cheese, egg, black pepper, and mustard into the Chopper Bowl fitted with the Chopper Blades.
4. Pulse using Speed Selector Button 2 until all of the ingredients are chopped to the same consistency.
5. On a cutting board, roll out the crescent roll dough and press dough into one large rectangle then divide into 24 equal squares.
6. Roll the dough into little balls then place in muffin tin.
7. Using a small shot glass or tamper, press each dough ball to make a well in the dough.
8. Fill dough ball wells with ham mixture and bake for 15 minutes or until golden brown.
9. Remove and serve.

★★★★★ CHAMPAGNE CAPER VINAIGRETTE

MAKES 2 CUPS

INGREDIENTS

For the Vinaigrette:
2/3 cup grapeseed oil
1/3 cup champagne vinegar
2 tablespoons lemon juice
1 small shallot, halved
1 garlic clove
1 tablespoon Dijon mustard
2 tablespoons capers, drained
2 teaspoons tarragon leaves
1/4 teaspoon kosher salt
1/4 teaspoon black pepper

For the Salad:
8 cups spring mix
1/2 cup Feta cheese, crumbled
1/2 cup dried cranberries
1/2 cup candied pecans

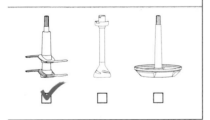

METHOD

1. Place all vinaigrette ingredients in the order listed into the Chopper Bowl fitted with the Chopper Blades.
2. Press Speed Selector Button 2 for 20 seconds or until all ingredients are chopped and the oil and vinegar are emulsified.
3. In a salad bowl, toss together all salad ingredients with 1/2 cup vinaigrette then serve with remaining vinaigrette on the side.

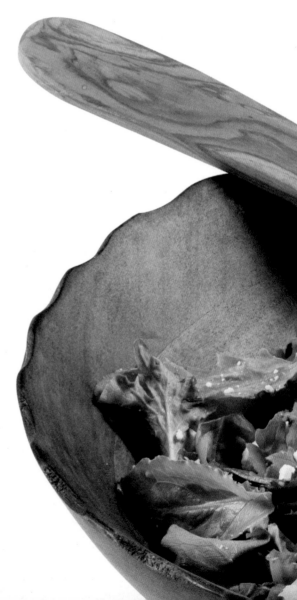

35

★★★★★
MINI CHICKEN BURGERS

=== **MAKES 4 SERVINGS** ===

INGREDIENTS

2 raw boneless skinless chicken breasts

2 green onions, cut into 1-inch pieces

1 teaspoon dried Italian seasoning

1 garlic clove

Juice of 1 lemon

1 whole egg

1/4 cup panko or plain breadcrumbs

1/2 teaspoon paprika

1/4 teaspoon kosher salt

1/4 teaspoon ground pepper

1 tablespoon grapeseed oil

Whole wheat slider buns

METHOD

1. Place all ingredients, except oil and buns, in the order listed into the Chopper Bowl fitted with the Chopper Blades.
2. Pulse using Speed Selector Button 2 until desired consistency is achieved.
3. Divide mixture into eight 2-ounce patties.
4. Preheat the grapeseed oil in a large skillet over medium heat.
5. Add patties to skillet and cook on medium heat for 3 minutes on each side or until internal temperature reaches 165°F on a meat thermometer.
6. Serve as desired on buns.

★★★★★ FROZEN MARGARITA

MAKES 1 SERVING

INGREDIENTS

2 cups ice

2 ounces orange-flavored liqueur

1 whole lime, peeled

1 ounce tequila

1 1/2 tablespoons caster sugar
(page 51)

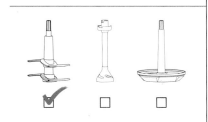

METHOD

1. Place all ingredients in the order listed into the Chopper Bowl fitted with the Chopper Blades.

2. Press Speed Selector Button 2 for 20 seconds, pause for a few seconds then pulse using Speed Selector Button 2 until all of the ice is crushed evenly.

3. Pour into glass, garnish as desired and serve immediately.

★★★★★
ASPARAGUS & RICOTTA PIZZA

=== **MAKES 1 PIZZA** ===

INGREDIENTS

For the Dough:
1/2 cup warm water

1 1/2 teaspoons active dry yeast

1/2 teaspoon sugar

1 tablespoon grapeseed oil

1 1/2 cups all purpose flour

1/2 teaspoon kosher salt

Cornmeal for
dusting baking sheet

For the Topping:
1 cup ricotta cheese

1/4 cup Parmesan cheese, grated

1 teaspoon garlic powder

1 pound asparagus (medium
thickness)

2 teaspoons grapeseed oil

METHOD

1. Preheat oven to 400°F.

2. In a measuring cup, combine the warm water, yeast, sugar and grapeseed oil; set aside and let rest for 10 minutes.

3. Generously dust a clean, dry work surface or cutting board with flour.

4. Place the flour and salt into the Chopper Bowl fitted with the Chopper Blades then add the yeast mixture.

5. Press Speed Selector Button 2 for up to 30 seconds until a dough ball is formed.

6. Shape dough into one smooth ball or 2 smaller balls to make 2 smaller pizzas.

7. On a lightly floured surface, pat dough into a flat disk then cover with a kitchen towel or cheese cloth and let rest for 30 minutes.

8. To make the topping, mix together the ricotta cheese, Parmesan and garlic powder in a bowl.

9. Using a vegetable peeler, shave the asparagus lengthwise into thin ribbons.

10. In a small bowl toss the asparagus ribbons with 2 teaspoons grapeseed oil.

11. After the dough has rested for 30 minutes, stretch the dough until 12 inches in diameter or 6 inches each if making two pizzas.

12. Sprinkle cornmeal on a baking sheet then add the stretched pizza dough.

13. Top dough with the ricotta mixture and asparagus ribbons.

14. Bake at 400°F for 10-12 minutes or until the crust is golden brown then remove and serve.

TIP

As an alternative, try using the whole wheat pizza dough on page 48.

★★★★★ ROASTED ALMOND BUTTER

=== **MAKES 1 CUP** ===

INGREDIENTS

8 ounces roasted almonds
2 tablespoons honey
3 tablespoons grapeseed oil

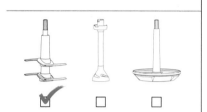

METHOD

1. Heat oven to 350°F.
2. Place roasted almonds on a cookie sheet and bake at 350°F for 6 minutes (this helps release the natural oils in the nuts).
3. Remove from oven then transfer almonds into the Chopper Bowl fitted with the Chopper Blades.
4. Pulse using Speed Selector Button 2 until almonds are chopped into small pieces then add remaining ingredients.
5. Press Speed Selector Button 2 for 30 seconds then carefully scrape down the sides of the Chopper Bowl and repeat until desired consistency is achieved (this process can take up to 3 minutes).
6. Serve as desired and store in the refrigerator for up to 3 months.

TIP

Heating the almonds shortens the processing time. You can also heat almonds in the microwave for 90 seconds.

ROASTED BEET HUMMUS

⭐⭐⭐⭐⭐

MAKES 4 SERVINGS

INGREDIENTS

2 garlic cloves, peeled

1/4 cup grapeseed oil

1 small beet, roasted (or use 1/2 cup jarred beets)

1 can (15 ounces) chickpeas, drained

Zest and juice of 1 lemon

1/8 teaspoon kosher salt

1/8 teaspoon black pepper

3 tablespoons tahini

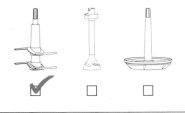

METHOD

1. Place the garlic and oil in a small sauce pot and simmer over medium heat until garlic is soft and golden brown; remove from heat and let cool to room temperature.
2. Transfer the oil and garlic as well as the remaining ingredients to the Chopper Bowl fitted with the Chopper Blades.
3. Press Speed Selector Button 2 for 20-30 seconds until all ingredients are smooth.
4. Serve hummus with your favorite fresh raw vegetables.

TIP

Hummus is a great replacement for dairy-based condiments.

★★★★★
GUACAMOLE

MAKES 2 CUPS

INGREDIENTS

2 ripe avocados, pitted and skinned

Juice of 2 limes

1 garlic clove

1 Campari tomato

1/4 red onion, cut into 1 1/2-inch pieces

1 tablespoon cilantro leaves

1/2 teaspoon roasted ground cumin

1 teaspoon sea salt

1/2 teaspoon cayenne pepper

METHOD

1. Place all ingredients into the Chopper Bowl fitted with the Chopper Blades.

2. Press Speed Selector Button 2 for 20 seconds then carefully scrape down the sides of the Chopper Bowl and repeat until desired consistency is achieved.

3. Serve as desired.

TIP

This is a great appetizer served with tortilla chips.

★★★★★
RASPBERRY POMEGRANATE
SORBET

=== MAKES 4 SERVINGS ===

INGREDIENTS

12 ounces frozen raspberries

1/2 cup pomegranate juice

1 cup caster sugar (page 51)

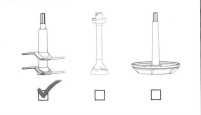

METHOD

1. Place all ingredients in the order listed into the Chopper Bowl fitted with the Chopper Blades.
2. Press Speed Selector Button 2 for 30 seconds then carefully scrape down the sides of the Chopper Bowl and repeat until smooth (this process can take up to 2 minutes).
3. Serve immediately.

TIP

You can substitute the frozen raspberries for frozen blueberries or blackberries.

★ ★ ★ ★ ★
PEACH MANGO POPSICLES
MAKES 2 SERVINGS

INGREDIENTS

8 ounces frozen mango

8 ounces frozen peaches

8 ounces mango juice

2 tablespoons caster sugar
(page 51)

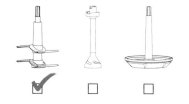

METHOD

1. Place all ingredients in the order listed into the Chopper Bowl fitted with the Chopper Blades.
2. Press Speed Selector Button 2 for 30 seconds or until mixture is smooth.
3. Fill popsicle molds with mixture 3/4 full to allow room for the mixture to expand as it freezes.
4. Freeze for 3-4 hours or until hardened and serve.

TIP

You can use paper cups filled 3/4 full. Stretch plastic wrap over the cups, cut a small whole in the center and insert a popsicle stick.

EGG SALAD LETTUCE WRAPS

★★★★★

— MAKES 2 SERVINGS —

INGREDIENTS

6 hardboiled eggs

1/4 cup mayonnaise

1 teaspoon store-bought
sriracha hot sauce

1 teaspoon paprika

1/4 teaspoon kosher salt

1/4 teaspoon black pepper

6 butter lettuce leaves
for serving

3 green onions, sliced (optional)

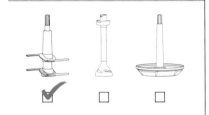

METHOD

1. Place the eggs, mayonnaise sriracha, paprika, salt and pepper into the Chopper Bowl fitted with the Chopper Blades.

2. Pulse using Speed Selector Button 1 until desired consistency is achieved (do not over process).

3. Spoon egg salad mixture onto lettuce leaves, top with green onions, garnish as desired and serve.

TIP
Add jalapeño if you
like it extra spicy.

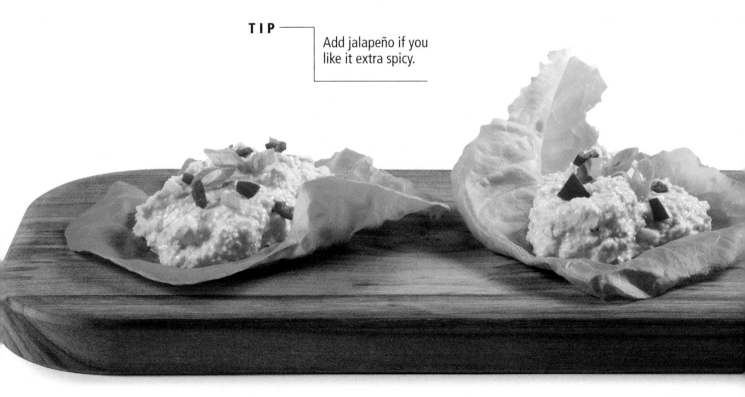

★★★★★ FROZEN MARTINI

MAKES 1 SERVING

INGREDIENTS

2 cups ice

2 ounces gin

1 ounce vodka

1 ounce olive juice from olive jar

Spanish olives for garnish

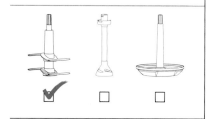

METHOD

1. Place all ingredients, except Spanish olives, in the order listed into the Chopper Bowl fitted with the Chopper Blades.
2. Press Speed Selector Button 2 for 20 seconds, pause for a few seconds then pulse using Speed Selector Button 2 until all of the ice is crushed evenly.
3. Pour into glass, garnish with olives and serve immediately.

★★★★★ Spinach Feta Crescent Rolls

MAKES 8 ROLLS

INGREDIENTS

2 cups baby spinach

1 garlic clove

1/2 cup mozzarella cheese, shredded

1/2 cup feta cheese, crumbled

1 egg, beaten

1/4 teaspoon red pepper flakes

1/8 teaspoon kosher salt

1/8 teaspoon black pepper

1 package (8 ounces) store-bought crescent rolls

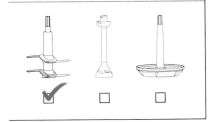

METHOD

1. Preheat oven to 350°F then apply nonstick cooking spray to a baking sheet; set aside.

2. Place all ingredients, except crescent rolls, into the Chopper Bowl fitted with the Chopper Blades.

3. Press Speed Selector Button 2 for 20 seconds or until all ingredients are combined.

4. Unroll the crescent dough, divide into triangles then place each piece on the baking sheet 2-inches apart.

5. Evenly divide the spinach mixture between the triangles, placing the mixture at the widest part of each triangle.

6. Roll up crescent dough tightly.

7. Bake for 15 minutes or until golden brown.

8. Remove and serve.

TIP

You can use parchment paper or nonstick foil instead of nonstick cooking spray.

★★★★★
WHOLE WHEAT PIZZA DOUGH

MAKES 1 PIZZA

INGREDIENTS

1/2 cup warm water

1/2 teaspoon active dry yeast

1/2 teaspoon honey

1/2 tablespoon grapeseed oil

1 cup whole wheat flour, plus more for kneading

1/2 teaspoon kosher salt

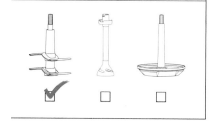

METHOD

1. Preheat oven to 350°F.
2. In a measuring cup measure 1/2 cup warm water then add the yeast, honey and grapeseed oil; stir well then set aside and let rest for 5 minutes.
3. Generously dust a clean, dry work surface or cutting board with flour.
4. Pour the flour and salt as well as the yeast mixture into the Chopper Bowl fitted with the Chopper Blades.
5. Press Speed Selector Button 2 for 30 seconds or until a dough ball is formed.
6. Transfer dough ball to a floured work surface.
7. Shape dough into one smooth ball then pat dough into a flat disk; cover with a kitchen towel or cheese cloth and let rest for 30 minutes.
8. To make a pizza, stretch the dough until it reaches 6-12 inches in diameter, depending on your desired thickness.
9. Top the dough with your favorite pizza toppings and bake on a sheet pan for 12-15 minutes at 350°F.
10. Serve immediately.

TROPICAL ICE CREAM

★ ★ ★ ★ ★

=== MAKES 4 SERVINGS ===

INGREDIENTS

1 can (13.66 ounces)
coconut milk

1/2 cup heavy cream

Zest and juice from 1 lime

16 ounces frozen pineapple

1/4 cup caster sugar (page 51)

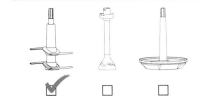

METHOD

1. Place all ingredients in the order listed into the Chopper Bowl fitted with the Chopper Blades.

2. Press Speed Selector Button 2 for 30 seconds, pause to let the pineapple chunks settle then scrape down the Chopper Bowl and repeat until smooth (this process can take up to 2 minutes).

3. Serve immediately.

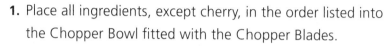

PURPLE SCHOOL BUS

INGREDIENTS

2 cups ice

1 cup grape juice

1 cup tart cherry juice

1 1/2 tablespoons caster sugar (page 51)

Maraschino cherry for garnish

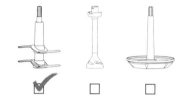

METHOD

1. Place all ingredients, except cherry, in the order listed into the Chopper Bowl fitted with the Chopper Blades.

2. Press Speed Selector Button 2 for 20 seconds, pause for a few seconds then pulse using Speed Selector Button 2 until all of the ice is crushed evenly.

3. Pour into glass, garnish with a cherry if desired and serve immediately.

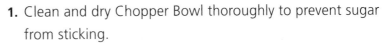

CASTER SUGAR

MAKES 1 CUP

INGREDIENTS

1 cup + 2 tablespoons
granulated sugar

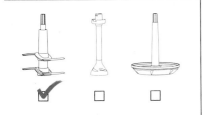

METHOD

1. Clean and dry Chopper Bowl thoroughly to prevent sugar from sticking.
2. Place sugar into the Chopper Bowl fitted with the Chopper Blades.
3. Press Speed Selector Button 2 for 30 seconds, pause for 15 seconds then repeat for another 30 seconds.
4. Wait for 5 minutes before removing the Chopper Bowl Cover to allow the fine sugar to settle.

TIP

Caster sugar is a superfine sugar that dissolves almost instantly. It is perfect for making meringue or sweetening cold drinks or desserts. You can substitute it for granulated sugar cup-for-cup.

51

★★★★★ TARTAR SAUCE

MAKES 1 CUP

INGREDIENTS

1/4 cup cornichon pickles

1 tablespoon capers, drained

1 small shallot, quartered

1 teaspoon fresh tarragon, chopped

1/4 cup fresh parsley sprigs

1 cup mayonnaise (page 78) or use store-bought

2 teaspoons freshly squeezed lemon juice

1 teaspoon Dijon mustard

1/2 teaspoon store-bought Worcestershire sauce

METHOD

1. Place the pickles, capers, shallot, tarragon and parsley into the Chopper Bowl fitted with the Chopper Blades.
2. Press Speed Selector Button 2 for 20 seconds or until all ingredients are chopped evenly.
3. Add remaining ingredients then press Speed Selector Button 1 until mixed well.
4. Serve as desired.

★★★★★
MELON BALL

INGREDIENTS

2 cups ice
2 ounces melon liqueur
1 ounce vodka
2 ounces orange juice

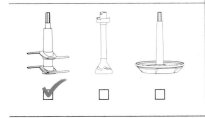

METHOD

1. Place all ingredients in the order listed into the Chopper Bowl fitted with the Chopper Blades.
2. Press Speed Selector Button 2 for 20 seconds, pause for a few seconds then pulse using Speed Selector Button 2 until all of the ice is crushed evenly.
3. Pour into glass, garnish as desired and serve immediately.

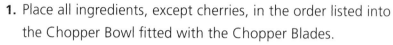

FROZEN CHERRY RUMBLE

MAKES 1 SERVING

INGREDIENTS

2 cups ice

1 ounce cherry rum

1 ounce melon liqueur

2 ounces cranberry juice

Maraschino cherries for garnish

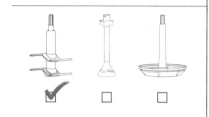

METHOD

1. Place all ingredients, except cherries, in the order listed into the Chopper Bowl fitted with the Chopper Blades.

2. Press Speed Selector Button 2 for 20 seconds, pause for a few seconds then pulse using Speed Selector Button 2 until all of the ice is crushed evenly.

3. Pour into glass, garnish with cherries and serve immediately.

MINI LEMON CHEESECAKES

★ ★ ★ ★ ★

MAKES 36 CAKES

INGREDIENTS

For the Crust:
18 vanilla wafers
Mini muffin tin
36 mini muffin paper liners

For the Batter:
2 packages (8 ounces each) cream cheese, room temperature
2/3 cup granulated sugar
Zest and juice of 1 lemon
2 large eggs
2 teaspoons vanilla extract

For the Glaze:
1 cup powdered sugar
Zest and juice from 1 lemon

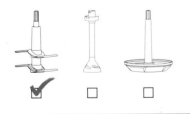

METHOD

1. Preheat oven to 325°F.
2. Place the vanilla wafers into the Chopper Bowl fitted with the Chopper Blades.
3. Press Speed Selector Button 2 for 15 seconds then transfer wafer crumbs to a mixing bowl; rinse and dry the Chopper Bowl and Chopper Blades.
4. Place all batter ingredients into the Chopper Bowl fitted with the Chopper Blades.
5. Press Speed Selector Button 2 for 20 seconds or until smooth and creamy (do not over process).
6. Place paper liners in each cup of the muffin tin then add 3/4 teaspoon vanilla wafer crumbs and top with 1 tablespoon cheesecake batter.
7. Bake in the oven at 325°F for 20 minutes or until cheesecakes are set then remove and let cool on a wire rack; repeat with remaining batter.
8. Rinse and dry the Chopper Bowl and Chopper Blades then add all glaze ingredients into the Chopper Bowl fitted with the Chopper Blades.
9. Press Speed Selector Button 1 for 20 seconds then transfer mixture to a measuring cup and refrigerate to set.
10. Refrigerate cooled cheesecakes for 4 hours then top with glaze and serve.

55

★★★★★
LEMON, LIME &
ORANGE GLAZES

MAKES 1 CUP

INGREDIENTS

For the Lemon Glaze:
2 cups powdered sugar
Zest and juice from 2 lemons

For the Lime Glaze:
2 cups powdered sugar
Zest and juice from 2 limes

For the Orange Glaze:
2 cups powdered sugar
Zest and juice from 1 orange

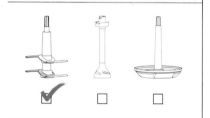

METHOD

1. Place desired glaze ingredients into the Chopper Bowl fitted with the Chopper Blades.
2. Press Speed Selector Button 2 for 20 seconds or until smooth.
3. Use the lemon glaze to top the mini lemon cheesecakes (page 55) and the lime or orange glazes to make a nice dipping sauce for sugar cookies.

★★★★★
AVOCADO VINAIGRETTE
MAKES 1 CUP

INGREDIENTS

1 ripe avocado, pitted and skinned

1 garlic clove

1/2 teaspoon kosher salt

Juice of 1 lime

2 tablespoons water

1 tablespoon rice wine vinegar

1/2 teaspoon bottled hot pepper sauce

6 tablespoons grapeseed oil

1/4 cup fresh cilantro leaves

1 Campari tomato

1/4 red onion, cut into 1 1/2-inch pieces

1 tablespoon cilantro leaves

METHOD

1. Place all ingredients into the Chopper Bowl fitted with the Chopper Blades.
2. Press Speed Selector Button 2 for 20 seconds then scrape down the Chopper bowl using a rubber spatula and process for another 20 seconds or until desired consistency.
3. Serve with your favorite salad or use as a dip for fresh cut vegetables.

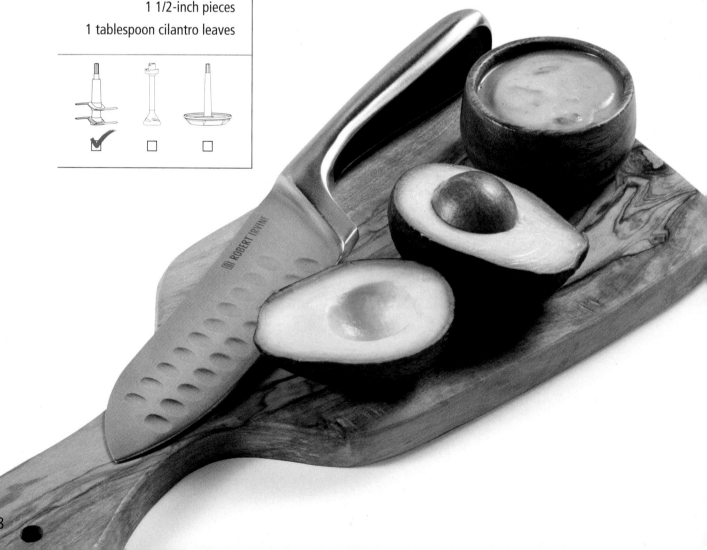

★★★★★
BUTTERNUT SQUASH SOUP

MAKES 4 SERVINGS

INGREDIENTS

2 garlic cloves

1 coin ginger

1 small yellow onion, cut into 1-inch pieces

1 tablespoon grapeseed oil

4 cups butternut squash, cubed

5 cups chicken stock

1 tablespoon kosher salt

2 teaspoons black pepper

2 tablespoons brown sugar

1 cup heavy cream

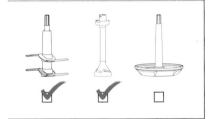

METHOD

1. Place the garlic, ginger and onions into the Chopper Bowl fitted with the Chopper Blades.
2. Pulse using Speed Selector Button 2 until chopped (do not over process).
3. Preheat the oil in a large stockpot over medium heat.
4. Sauté the onion mixture for 3 minutes, stirring often, or until onions are clear.
5. Add remaining ingredients, except heavy cream then bring to a boil.
6. Reduce heat and simmer uncovered for 30 minutes or until butternut squash is fork tender.
7. Using the Blending Rod inserted into the bottom of the stockpot, puree with Speed Selector Button 1 until smooth (do not remove the Blending Rod from the pot while running to avoid splatter).
8. Add the heavy cream and continue blending until creamy.
9. Garnish as desired and serve.

TIP

Most grocery stores sell butternut squash already precut.

59

FROZEN GIN & JUICE

★★★★★

===== **MAKES 1 SERVING** =====

INGREDIENTS

2 cups ice

3 ounces gin

1 ounce triple sec

1 ounce freshly
squeezed lime juice

1 ounce simple syrup

Juice from 1 orange

Orange peel for garnish

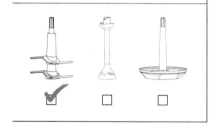

METHOD

1. Place all ingredients, except orange peel, in the order listed into the Chopper Bowl fitted with the Chopper Blades.

2. Press Speed Selector Button 2 for 20 seconds, pause for a few seconds then pulse using Speed Selector Button 2 until all of the ice is crushed evenly.

3. Pour into glass, garnish with orange peel and serve immediately.

HAM SALAD SANDWICH

★ ★ ★ ★ ★

MAKES 4 SERVINGS

INGREDIENTS

2 cups diced ham (or one 16-ounce ham steak cut into 1-inch pieces)

1/4 yellow onion, cut into 1-inch pieces

1/2 cup mayonnaise

1 tablespoon yellow mustard

1/4 cup sweet pickle relish

1/4 teaspoon kosher salt

1/2 teaspoon black pepper

4 butter lettuce leaves

4 kaiser rolls

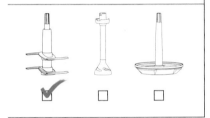

METHOD

1. Place all ingredients, except lettuce and rolls, in the order listed into the Chopper Bowl fitted with the Chopper Blades.

2. Pulse using Speed Selector Button 2 until desired consistency is achieved.

3. Serve on kaiser rolls with lettuce and desired garnish.

TIP

Great served on crackers as an appetizer.

★★★★★ CHICKEN TACOS WITH AVOCADO LIME DRESSING

MAKES 2 SERVINGS

INGREDIENTS

For the Dressing:

1/2 cup sour cream

1 ripe avocado, pitted and skinned

1/4 cup cilantro leaves

Juice of 1 large lime

1 jalapeño pepper, seeds removed and sliced

1 teaspoon kosher salt

For the Tacos:

1 1/2 teaspoons smoked paprika

1 teaspoon garlic powder

1 teaspoon dried oregano

1 teaspoon onion powder

1/2 teaspoon cumin

1/2 teaspoon kosher salt

1/2 teaspoon brown sugar

1/4 teaspoon cayenne pepper

2 boneless, skinless chicken breasts, cut into thin strips

1 tablespoon grapeseed oil

6 corn tortillas

2 cups romaine lettuce, chopped

1/4 red onion, thinly sliced

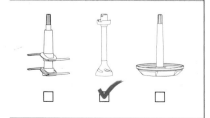

METHOD

1. Place all dressing ingredients in the order listed into a tall, narrow container.

2. Using the Blending Rod, blend with Speed Selector Button 2 for 20-30 seconds until smooth; set aside.

3. Preheat a large skillet over medium heat for 5 minutes.

4. In a large bowl, combine the paprika, garlic powder, oregano, onion powder, cumin, salt, brown sugar and cayenne pepper.

5. Place the chicken on a cutting board then sprinkle with the paprika mixture.

6. Pour the oil into the skillet and let heat for 1 minute.

7. Add the chicken strips to the pan and sauté for 3-4 minutes or until chicken is no longer pink and juices run clean; transfer to a serving dish.

8. Using the same skillet, heat the corn tortillas for 15 seconds on each side.

9. Divide the cooked chicken between the corn tortillas then top with lettuce, red onions, avocado lime dressing and desired garnish before serving.

★ ★ ★ ★ ★

TIP

You can substitute
the chicken for
shrimp or your
favorite white fish
if you desire.

Mustard-Herb Vinaigrette

★ ★ ★ ★ ★

MAKES 1 CUP

INGREDIENTS

1/2 cup grapeseed oil

1/4 cup white wine vinegar

1 hard cooked egg yolk

1 tablespoon grainy mustard

1 tablespoon Dijon mustard

1 garlic clove

1/2 teaspoon kosher salt

1/2 teaspoon black pepper

2 teaspoons fresh tarragon leaves

2 teaspoons chervil (or use basil or parsley if desired)

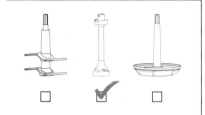

METHOD

1. Place all ingredients in the order listed into a tall, narrow container.
2. With the Blending Rod at the bottom of the container, press Speed Selector Button 2 while keeping the rod in place for 10 seconds.
3. Begin moving the Blending Rod up and down for 20-30 seconds until the ingredients are completely emulsified.
4. Serve over your favorite salad.

★ ★ ★ ★ ★

WATERMELON SLUSHY

MAKES 2 SERVINGS

INGREDIENTS

3 cups watermelon cubes, cut
into 1-inch squares and frozen

1 cup red grapes

2 tablespoons agave syrup

Zest and juice from 2 limes

1/2 cup coconut water

METHOD

1. Place all ingredients in the order listed into a tall, narrow container.

2. Place the Blending Rod at the top of the ingredients in the container then blend using Speed Selector Button 2 while pressing down until the ingredients start to blend. Move rod up and down for 20-30 seconds until completely blended.

3. Divide between two glasses and serve.

TIP

Try substituting cantaloupe or honeydew with green grapes for other refreshing drinks.

★★★★★
PEA SOUP

═══ MAKES 4 SERVINGS ═══

INGREDIENTS

1 tablespoon grapeseed oil
1 small shallot, chopped
1 garlic clove, chopped
3 cups vegetable stock
4 cups frozen peas
1 teaspoon salt
1 teaspoon black pepper

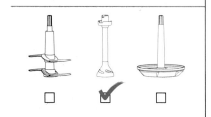

METHOD

1. Preheat a 3-quart stockpot over medium-high heat.
2. Add the grapeseed oil and heat for 1 minute.
3. Add the shallots and cook for 2 minutes, stirring constantly, or until shallots begin to brown.
4. Add the garlic and sauté for 1 minute or until garlic begins to brown.
5. Add remaining ingredients and bring to a boil.
6. Reduce heat to a simmer, cook for 5 minutes uncovered while stirring occasionally then remove from heat.
7. Using the Blending Rod inserted into the bottom of the stockpot, puree with Speed Selector Button 1 for 30 seconds or until smooth (do not remove the Blending Rod from the pot while running to avoid splatter).
8. Garnish as desired and serve hot.

TIP

Pea soup is excellent served cold in the summer time.

★★★★★
Buttermilk
Ranch Dressing
MAKES 2 CUPS

INGREDIENTS

3/4 cup buttermilk

1/2 cup sour cream

1/2 cup mayonnaise

2 garlic cloves

1 tablespoon fresh parsley leaves

1 teaspoon fresh dill

1 teaspoon chives, chopped

1/2 teaspoon onion powder

1/2 teaspoon kosher salt

2 teaspoons lemon juice

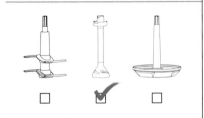

METHOD

1. Place all ingredients in the order listed into a tall, narrow container.

2. Using the Blending Rod, blend with Speed Selector Button 2 while moving the rod up and down for 20-30 seconds until smooth.

3. Serve over your favorite salad or as dipping sauce for fresh vegetables.

★★★★★ CREAMY COLESLAW

MAKES 1 CUP

INGREDIENTS

For the Dressing:

1 cup grapeseed oil

1/4 cup + 2 tablespoons white wine vinegar

2 large egg yolks

1 1/4 teaspoons kosher salt

1/4 teaspoon black pepper

1 tablespoon Dijon mustard

1 teaspoon celery seed

1/4 cup sugar

For the Coleslaw:

4 cups green cabbage, shredded

2 cups purple cabbage, shredded

1 cup carrots, shredded

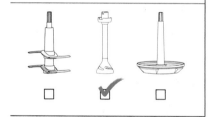

METHOD

1. Place all dressing ingredients in the order listed into a tall, narrow container.
2. With the Blending Rod at the bottom of the container, press Speed Selector Button 2 while keeping the rod in place for 10 seconds.
3. Begin moving the Blending Rod up and down until the ingredients are completely emulsified.
4. In a large bowl combine all coleslaw ingredients.
5. Add the dressing, mix well then refrigerate until ready to serve.

TIP

For quick coleslaw you can purchase prepackaged shredded cabbage at your local grocery store. The dressing can be made in advance and kept in the refrigerator for up to one week.

★★★★★ BABY FOOD

MAKES 1 CUP

INGREDIENTS	METHOD

INGREDIENTS

Pea:

1 cup frozen peas

1/2 cup water

Peach:

1 cup frozen peaches

1/2 cup water

Carrot:

1 cup carrots, steamed until fork tender

1/2 cup water

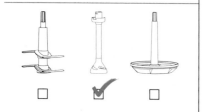

METHOD

1. Place desired vegetable or fruit ingredients into a tall, narrow container.
2. Using the Blending Rod, blend with Speed Selector Button 1 for 20-30 seconds until smooth.
3. Serve immediately.

TIP

You can double the recipe and freeze in ice cube trays for future use.

HOMEMADE APPLESAUCE

★ ★ ★ ★ ★

MAKES 2 CUPS

INGREDIENTS

4 medium apples, cored, peeled and cut into 1/4-inch pieces

3/4 cups apple juice, divided

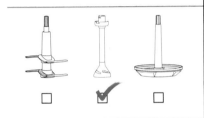

METHOD

1. Combine the apples and 1/2 cup apple juice in a 3-quart saucepot.
2. Cook over medium-high heat for 10 minutes or until fork tender.
3. Remove from heat then add remaining apple juice to the saucepot.
4. Using the Blending Rod, blend with Speed Selector Button 2 while moving the rod up and down for 30 seconds, then stop for 20 seconds to let apples settle and repeat until desired consistency is achieved.
5. Let mixture cool to room temperature then refrigerate until ready to eat.

TIP
Try adding cinnamon for added flavor.

★★★★★
CHEESE BLINTZES
MAKES 4 SERVINGS

INGREDIENTS

For the Crepe Batter:
1 cup water
3/4 cup whole milk
3 large eggs
5 tablespoons unsalted butter, melted
1/2 teaspoon kosher salt
1 1/2 cups all-purpose flour

For the Filling:
2 cups ricotta cheese
8 ounces cream cheese, softened
3/4 cup powdered sugar
Juice and zest of 1 lemon
1 egg

For Serving:
Powdered sugar

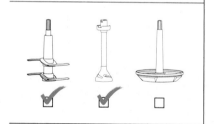

METHOD

1. Preheat a 10-inch nonstick skillet over medium heat.
2. Place all batter ingredients into a tall, narrow container.
3. Using the Blending Rod, blend with Speed Selector Button 1 while moving the rod up and down for 20-30 seconds until smooth and no lumps remain. You may need to scrape the sides of the container halfway through the process to make sure all of the flour is incorporated.
4. Lightly apply nonstick spray to the skillet then pour 1/4 cup of batter into the middle of the skillet.
5. Tilt skillet in a circular motion until the batter is evenly spread across the skillet. Cook for 1 minute on each side or until golden brown then transfer to a rack to cool. Repeat with remaining batter.
6. Place all filling ingredients into the Chopper Bowl fitted with the Chopper Blades.
7. Press Speed Selector Button 2 for 20 seconds or until smooth and creamy.
8. Once the crepes have cooled, place 1/4 cup of cheese filling in the center of each crepe, fold in the edges and roll.
9. Sprinkle with powdered sugar and serve.

TIP

The blintz filling is excellent in stuffed French toast as well. Follow the directions for the French toast on page 98 then use a paring knife to cut through the bottom crust of each bread slice horizontally. This creates a pocket to stuff with this blintz filling.

★★★★★
QUICK MARINARA SAUCE

MAKES 7 CUPS

INGREDIENTS

1 teaspoon grapeseed oil

3 garlic cloves

2 cans (28 ounces each) plum tomatoes

1 teaspoon fresh oregano

1 teaspoon fresh basil

1/4 teaspoon crushed red pepper flakes

1 teaspoon kosher salt

1 teaspoon black pepper

1 teaspoon granulated sugar

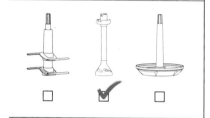

METHOD

1. Preheat the oil in a 3-quart stockpot over medium heat.
2. Add the garlic and sauté until golden brown.
3. Add remaining ingredients and cook over medium heat for 10 minutes then remove from heat.
4. Using the Blending Rod, puree with Speed Selector Button 1 while moving the rod up and down until smooth (do not remove the Blending Rod from the pot while running or tilt the rod too close to the surface to avoid splatter).
5. Serve as dipping sauce for bread sticks or over your favorite cooked pasta.

TIP

Freeze extra sauce in an airtight container for up to 6 months. You can also use this marinara sauce as pizza sauce with the pizza dough recipe on page 48.

★ ★ ★ ★ ★

Sriracha Aioli

MAKES 1 CUP

INGREDIENTS

1 cup grapeseed oil

3 tablespoons white vinegar

1 1/4 teaspoons kosher salt

1/4 teaspoon white pepper

1 tablespoon Dijon mustard

2 tablespoons store-bought sriracha hot sauce

2 tablespoons store-bought sweet chili sauce

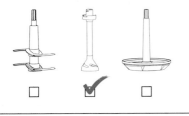

METHOD

1. Place all ingredients in the order listed into a tall, narrow container.
2. With the Blending Rod at the bottom of the container, press Speed Selector Button 2 while keeping the rod in place for 10 seconds then begin moving the rod up and down for 20 seconds or until ingredients are completely emulsified.
3. Aioli can be stored in an airtight container in the refrigerator for up to one week.

TIP

This makes an excellent sandwich spread as well as a condiment for fish or shrimp.

★★★★★ CHOCOLATE COCONUT BREAD PUDDING

MAKES 6 SERVINGS

INGREDIENTS

5 eggs

1/2 cup sugar

1 1/8 cup milk

1 1/8 cup heavy cream

1 teaspoon vanilla extract

1 loaf brioche or 1 challah, cut into 1-inch cubes

1/2 cup pecans, chopped

3/4 cup coconut, shredded

3 1/2 ounces bittersweet chocolate, grated

3 tablespoons unsalted butter, cut into small pieces

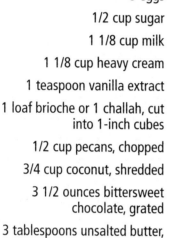

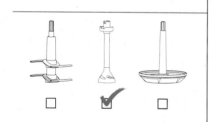

METHOD

1. Place eggs, sugar, milk, heavy cream and vanilla into a tall, narrow container.
2. Using the Blending Rod, blend with Speed Selector Button 1 for 20 seconds or until smooth.
3. Apply nonstick cooking spray to an oven-safe 10-inch sauté pan.
4. Arrange half of the cubed challah in the bottom of the pan then scatter half of the pecans, coconut and chocolate over the bread. Top with remaining challah pieces as well as remaining pecans, coconut and chocolate.
5. Pour the batter over the bread cubes in the pan, top with butter pieces and let stand for 30 minutes.
6. Preheat oven to 300°F.
7. Place the sauté pan in the oven and cook for 40 minutes or until the pudding is just firm.
8. Remove from oven, garnish as desired and serve hot.

TIP

Excellent served with toasted coconut over the top.

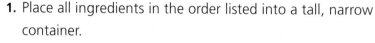

★★★★★ MAYONNAISE

MAKES 1 CUP

INGREDIENTS

1 cup grapeseed oil
3 tablespoons white vinegar
2 large egg yolks
1 1/4 teaspoons kosher salt
1/4 teaspoon white pepper
1 tablespoon Dijon mustard

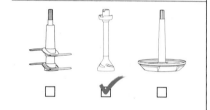

METHOD

1. Place all ingredients in the order listed into a tall, narrow container.

2. With the Blending Rod at the bottom of the container, press Speed Selector Button 2 while keeping the rod in place for 10 seconds then begin moving the rod up and down for 20 seconds or until ingredients are completely emulsified.

3. Mayonnaise can be stored in an airtight container in the refrigerator for up to one week.

TIP

You can make flavored mayonnaise by adding fresh herbs or a tablespoon of basil pesto on page 10.

★★★★★
MANGO LASSI
═══ MAKES 2 SERVINGS ═══

INGREDIENTS

2 cups frozen mango
2 cups low-fat vanilla yogurt
1/4 cup heavy cream or milk
1/2 teaspoon cardamom powder
4 tablespoons honey

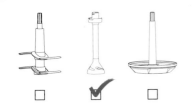

METHOD

1. Place all ingredients in the order listed into a tall, narrow container.
2. With the Blending Rod at the top of the container, press Speed Selector Button 2 while pressing down on the ingredients until you reach the bottom.
3. Begin moving the Blending Rod up and down for 20 seconds or until the ingredients are completely emulsified.
4. Divide between 2 glasses and serve.

★★★★★ RASPBERRY & BLACKBERRY JAM

MAKES 4-6 CUPS

INGREDIENTS

For the Raspberry Jam:

6 cups frozen
raspberries, thawed

5 1/4 cups caster sugar
(page 51)

1 package (3 ounces) liquid
fruit pectin

For the Blackberry Jam:

4 cups frozen
blackberries, thawed

4 cups caster sugar (page 51)

1 package (3 ounces) liquid
fruit pectin

3 jelly or mason jars
(8 ounces each)

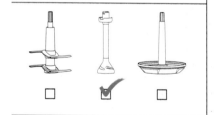

METHOD

1. Place all ingredients for either the raspberry or blackberry jam into a tall, narrow container.

2. Using the Blending Rod, blend with Speed Selector Button 2 for 30 seconds or until smooth.

3. Immediately pour into jelly or mason jars, leaving 1/2-inch space from the top of the jar to allow for expansion if freezing the jam.

4. Refrigerate until ready to use.

5. Freeze any unused jam for up to 6 months. Thaw and stir prior to serving.

★ ★ ★ ★ ★

TIP

For Strawberry jam, use 4 cups frozen strawberries, 3 1/2 cups sugar, and one package fruit pectin. These jams are delicious on toast, ice cream or even in milkshakes!

★ ★ ★ ★ ★
FRUIT LEATHER

=== **MAKES 8-12 SERVINGS** ===

INGREDIENTS

3 cups fresh raspberries

1/2 cup apple juice

1/2 cup powdered sugar

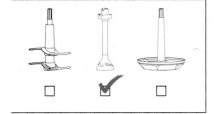

METHOD

1. Preheat oven to 170°F.

2. Cut a piece of parchment paper slightly larger than your cookie sheet and set aside.

3. Apply nonstick spray to the cookie sheet then place the parchment paper on top of the nonstick spray to keep it in place. Make sure to leave 1/2-inch of parchment paper around the sides of the cookie sheet to keep the mixture contained.

4. Place all ingredients in the order listed into a tall, narrow container.

5. Using the Blending Rod, blend with Speed Selector Button 2 while moving the rod up and down for 30 seconds or until completely liquified.

6. Pour mixture onto the prepared cookie sheet (strain first to remove seeds if desired) then tilt the cookie sheet in different directions until the bottom of the sheet is covered with the mixture.

7. Place in the oven for 2 hours or until the fruit is no longer damp to the touch. Remove and let cool.

8. Cut the fruit leather into strips using scissors and store in an airtight container at room temperature for up to 1 week.

TIP ──┐
Substitute the raspberries with any other berry or fruit and adjust sugar to taste.

★★★★★ HONEY CLOUD PANCAKE

MAKES 2 SERVINGS

INGREDIENTS

2 large egg whites

2 large whole eggs

1/2 cup milk

1/2 cup all-purpose flour

1/4 teaspoon kosher salt

2 teaspoons honey, plus more for serving

2 teaspoons vanilla extract

1 tablespoon unsalted butter

1/2 cup fresh fruit or berries such as raspberries, blueberries or blackberries for serving

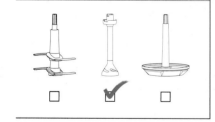

METHOD

1. Preheat oven to 400°F.

2. Preheat an oven-safe 10-inch nonstick sauté pan over medium-low heat for 5 minutes.

3. Place the egg whites into a 2-cup measuring cup with a wide bottom.

4. In a separate tall container or 4-cup measuring cup, place the whole eggs, milk, flour, salt, 2 teaspoons honey and vanilla.

5. Using the Blending Rod, blend egg whites with Speed Selector Button 1 for 25 seconds or until they triple in size.

6. Using the Blending Rod, blend the whole egg mixture with Speed Selector Button 1 for 10 seconds or until smooth without any lumps remaining.

7. Pour the egg white mixture into the whole egg mixture then fold together using a rubber spatula.

8. Melt the butter in the preheated sauté pan then pour in the pancake mixture and cook over medium heat until the sides begin to firm.

9. Place the sauté pan in the oven and bake at 400°F for 8 minutes.

10. Remove from oven and transfer to a cutting board then cut into 8 slices.

11. Top with additional honey and berries before serving.

★★★★★
BBQ Chicken Kabobs

MAKES 4 SERVINGS

INGREDIENTS

For the BBQ Sauce:

1 teaspoon grapeseed oil

1/2 teaspoon onion powder

1/2 teaspoon garlic powder

1 cup ketchup

1/4 cup brown sugar

2/3 cup white wine vinegar

1 tablespoon Worcestershire sauce

1 tablespoon yellow mustard

1/3 cup apple cider vinegar

1 teaspoons kosher salt

1/4 teaspoon cayenne pepper

1/4 cup bacon bits

1 1/2 tablespoons molasses

For the Chicken Kabobs:

2 pounds raw boneless, skinless chicken breast, cut into 1-inch pieces

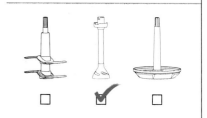

METHOD

1. Place all BBQ sauce ingredients in the order listed into a tall, narrow container.

2. Using the Blending Rod, blend with Speed Selector Button 2 for 20 seconds or until mixed well.

3. Coat the chicken with half of the sauce in a mixing bowl (reserve remaining sauce for serving).

4. Preheat a large skillet over medium heat then apply nonstick cooking spray.

5. Once coated, divide the chicken pieces between eight 6-inch skewers.

6. Cook the chicken for 2 minutes on each side until chicken is browned and internal temperature reaches 165°F on a meat thermometer.

7. Remove from heat and serve with reserved BBQ Sauce.

★ ★ ★ ★ ★

TIP

Excellent served with the creamy coleslaw on page 68. This BBQ sauce recipe can be used on beef and pork as well.

FRESH FRUIT CREPES

★ ★ ★ ★ ★

MAKES 4 SERVINGS

INGREDIENTS

For the Batter:

1 cup water

3/4 cup whole milk

3 large eggs

5 tablespoons unsalted butter, melted

1/2 teaspoon kosher salt

1 1/2 cups all-purpose flour

For the Filling:

2 cups low-fat vanilla yogurt, divided

2 cups fresh mixed berries, divided

For Serving:

Powdered sugar

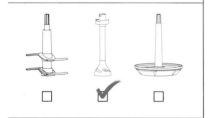

METHOD

1. Preheat a 10-inch nonstick skillet over medium heat.

2. Place all batter ingredients into a tall, narrow container.

3. Using the Blending Rod, blend with Speed Selector Button 1 while moving the rod up and down for 20-30 seconds until smooth and no lumps remain. You may need to scrape the sides of the container halfway through the process to make sure all of the flour is incorporated.

4. Lightly apply nonstick spray to the skillet then pour 1/4 cup of batter into the middle of the skillet.

5. Tilt skillet in a circular motion until the batter is evenly spread across the skillet. Cook for 1 minute on each side or until golden brown then transfer to a rack to cool. Repeat with remaining batter.

6. Once the crepes have cooled, place 1/4 cup of yogurt and 1/4 cup berries in the center of each crepe then fold in half then in half again to form triangles.

7. Sprinkle with powdered sugar and serve.

TIP

To make Chocolate crepes, add 3 tablespoons cocoa powder to the batter.

★★★★★
BUTTERMILK PANCAKES

MAKES 4 SERVINGS

INGREDIENTS

3 cups all purpose flour

3 tablespoons sugar

3 teaspoons baking powder

1 1/2 teaspoons baking soda

3/4 teaspoon salt

3 cups buttermilk

1/2 cup whole milk

3 eggs

2 tablespoons unsalted butter, melted

Maple Syrup for serving

4 tablespoons unsalted butter for serving

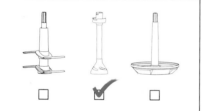

METHOD

1. Preheat a 10-inch nonstick sauté pan over medium-low heat for 5 minutes.
2. Place all ingredients except maple syrup and butter for serving into a large measuring cup or 2-quart pitcher.
3. Using the Blending Rod, blend with Speed Selector Button 2 for 30 seconds or until smooth.
4. Apply nonstick cooking spray to the sauté pan then add 1/2 cup batter for each pancake.
5. Cook for 2 minutes on each side or until browned then repeat with remaining batter.
6. Serve topped with maple syrup and butter.

RASPBERRY SMOOTHIE

★ ★ ★ ★ ★

MAKES 1 SERVING

INGREDIENTS

1/4 cup frozen raspberries

4 frozen strawberries

1 cup pomegranate juice

1 banana, sliced

1/4 cup Greek yogurt

2 tablespoons
vanilla protein powder

1/2 cup water

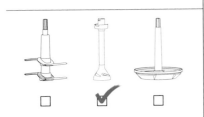

METHOD

1. Place all ingredients in the order listed into a tall, narrow container.
2. Using the Blending Rod, blend with Speed Selector Button 2 for 20 seconds or until smooth.
3. Serve immediately.

★★★★★
SUPERFOOD SMOOTHIE

MAKES 1 SERVING

INGREDIENTS

1/2 cup frozen honeydew melon, cut into 1/2-inch chunks

1/2 cup green grapes

1/2 cup kale (leaves only)

Juice from 1 lime

1/2 cup aloe juice

1 tablespoon green superfood protein powder

lemon lime powder

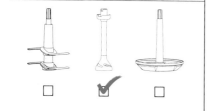

METHOD

1. Place all ingredients in the order listed into a tall, narrow container.
2. Using the Blending Rod, blend with Speed Selector Button 2 for 20 seconds or until smooth.
3. Serve immediately.

★★★★★ TOMATO SOUP

MAKES 2-4 SERVINGS

INGREDIENTS

1 teaspoon grapeseed oil

2 garlic cloves

1/2 small yellow onion, cut into 1/2-inch pieces

2 whole carrots, thinly sliced

1 can (28 ounces) whole tomatoes

1/2 teaspoon fresh thyme

3 cups vegetable stock

1/2 cup heavy cream or milk

1 1/2 tablespoons tomato paste

METHOD

1. Preheat the oil in a 3-quart stockpot over medium-high heat.
2. Add the garlic and onions, sauté until softened then add remaining ingredients and cook uncovered over medium heat for 10 minutes, stirring often. Remove from heat.
3. Using the Blending Rod inserted into the bottom of the stockpot, puree with Speed Selector Button 1 until smooth (do not remove the Blending Rod from the pot while running to avoid splatter).
4. Garnish as desired and serve.

★ ★ ★ ★ ★
BREAKFAST STRATA
═══ MAKES 6 SERVINGS ═══

INGREDIENTS

For the Custard:

8 eggs

3 cups heavy cream

8 ounces diced ham

1 teaspoon kosher salt

1 teaspoon black pepper

1 cup Parmesan cheese, grated

For the Strata:

1 challah loaf, cubed

1/2 red bell pepper, diced

1/4 white onion

1 cup Swiss cheese, shredded

1 teaspoon bottled hot pepper sauce

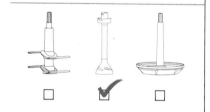

METHOD

1. Preheat oven to 350°F.

2. Place all custard ingredients in the order listed into a tall, narrow container.

3. Using the Blending Rod, blend with Speed Selector Button 2 for 20 seconds or until all ingredients are incorporated.

4. Apply nonstick cooking spray to a 10-inch casserole dish then add all strata ingredients in the order listed.

5. Pour custard over the ingredients in casserole dish and let soak for 15 minutes.

6. Place the casserole in the oven at 350°F and bake for 30 minutes or until the bread is toasted and the custard is set.

7. Remove and serve immediately.

★★★★★
GINGER LIME AIOLI

MAKES 1 CUP

INGREDIENTS

1 cup grapeseed oil

2 teaspoons freshly squeezed lime juice

2 whole eggs

1 egg yolk

1 teaspoon Dijon mustard

2 garlic cloves

1 coin ginger, cut into 4 pieces

1 teaspoon fine sea salt

1 teaspoon white pepper

METHOD

1. Place all ingredients in the order listed into a tall, narrow container.
2. With the Blending Rod at the bottom of the container, press Speed Selector Button 2 while keeping the rod in place for 10 seconds then begin moving the rod up and down until ingredients are completely emulsified.
3. Serve on your favorite sandwich or as desired.

TIP

Aioli can be kept in an airtight container in the refrigerator for up to one week.

PEACH MILKSHAKE

★ ★ ★ ★ ★

MAKES 2 SERVINGS

INGREDIENTS

2 cups frozen peaches

1 cup Greek vanilla yogurt

1 cup whole milk

2 tablespoons caster sugar
(page 51)

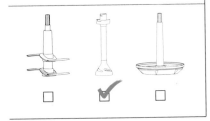

METHOD

1. Place all ingredients into a tall, narrow container.
2. With the Blending Rod at the top of the container, press Speed Selector Button 2 while pressing down on the ingredients until you reach the bottom.
3. Begin moving the Blending Rod up and down for 20 seconds or until the ingredients are completely emulsified.
4. Divide between 2 glasses and serve immediately.

TIP

You can substitute the peaches with any frozen fruit using the same ingredients. Adjust the sugar amount to taste based on the sweetness of the fruit used.

★★★★★ FRENCH TOAST

MAKES 4 SERVINGS

INGREDIENTS

For the Custard:

1 1/2 cups half & half

4 large whole eggs

2 tablespoons sugar

1 tablespoon vanilla extract

1/4 teaspoon ground cinnamon

For the French Toast:

1 loaf challah, cut into
8 slices, 1/2-inch thick each

4 tablespoons unsalted butter,
divided

2 cups of fresh fruit or berries
(such as raspberries, blueberries
and blackberries)

Maple Syrup or powdered sugar
for serving

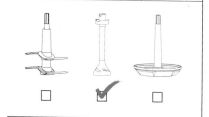

METHOD

1. Preheat a 10-inch nonstick sauté pan over medium-low heat for 5 minutes.

2. Place all custard ingredients into a tall, narrow container.

3. Using the Blending Rod, blend with Speed Selector Button 1 for 10 seconds or until smooth.

4. Transfer custard to a large bowl then dip the bread slices into the mixture for 30 seconds until all sides are coated.

5. Place 1 tablespoon of butter into the heated pan then add 2 soaked bread slices at a time and cook for 2-3 minutes on each side or until bread pieces are brown in color. Repeat with remaining butter and bread slices.

6. Serve with berries and maple syrup or sprinkle with powdered sugar if desired.

TIP

This recipe is also excellent made with English muffin bread or home-style bread purchased from the bakery at your local grocery store. Just ask them for an unsliced loaf and use in place of the challah.

★★★★★
GOAT CHEESE &
TOMATO DRESSING

MAKES 2 CUPS

INGREDIENTS

1/4 cup goat cheese, crumbled

1/4 cup white wine vinegar

2 teaspoons honey

1/2 cup grapeseed oil

1 cup cherry tomatoes, halved

1 tablespoon fresh
tarragon leaves

1/2 teaspoon kosher salt

METHOD

1. Place all ingredients in the order listed into a tall, narrow container.

2. Using the Blending Rod, blend with Speed Selector Button 2 while moving the rod up and down for 20-30 seconds or until smooth.

3. Serve over your favorite salad or as dipping sauce for fresh vegetables.

FROTHY HOT CHOCOLATE

MAKES 4 SERVINGS

INGREDIENTS

For the Hot Chocolate:

2 cups heavy cream

2 cups whole milk

8 ounces semi-sweet chocolate chips

1/2 teaspoon vanilla

4 teaspoons granulated sugar

For the Froth:

3/4 cup skim milk

2 tablespoons powdered sugar

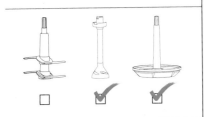

METHOD

1. In a medium saucepot, heat the heavy cream and whole milk over medium heat for 5 minutes, stirring occasionally.
2. Add the chocolate chips, vanilla and sugar then stir for 1 minute or until all of the chips are melted.
3. Using the Blending Rod, blend milk mixture with Speed Selector Button 1 for 30 seconds or until foamy. Reduce heat to simmer.
4. While the hot chocolate is keeping warm, place all froth ingredients into the Chopper Bowl fitted with the Emulsifying Disc.
5. Press Speed Selector Button 2 for 20 seconds.
6. Pour hot chocolate into mugs, top with froth, garnish as desired and serve.

TIP

Omit the sugar from the froth ingredients to save calories.

★★★★★ CAPRESE SALAD

══ MAKES 4 SERVINGS ══

INGREDIENTS

For the Dressing:

3/4 cup grapeseed oil

1/4 cup balsamic vinegar

1 teaspoon Dijon mustard

1 1/2 teaspoons honey

1/2 teaspoon kosher salt

1/2 teaspoon black pepper

For the Salad:

2 vine ripe tomatoes, sliced
1/4-inch thick

2 yellow tomatoes, sliced
1/4-inch thick

2 fresh mozzarella balls, sliced
into 4 pieces each

8 basil leaves

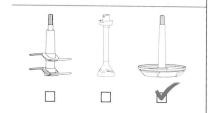

METHOD

1. Place all dressing ingredients into the Chopper Bowl fitted with the Emulsifying Disc.

2. Press Speed Selector Button 2 for 15 seconds or until well blended.

3. On a serving platter, layer all salad ingredients then top with dressing and serve.

4. Dressing can be kept in an airtight container in the refrigerator for up to two weeks.

★ ★ ★ ★ ★

TIP

Serve as an appetizer over cherry tomatoes and mini mozzarella ball skewers.

★★★★★
LEMON VINAIGRETTE

MAKES 1 CUP

INGREDIENTS

For the Vinaigrette:

1 cup grapeseed oil

1/4 cup white wine vinegar

2 teaspoons honey

1 teaspoon kosher salt

1/4 teaspoon white pepper

Zest and juice from 2 whole lemons

For the Salad:

2 cups arugula

1/4 cup raspberries

2 tablespoons candied pecans

1 radish, sliced

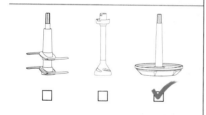

METHOD

1. Place all vinaigrette ingredients into the Chopper Bowl fitted with the Emulsifying Disc.

2. Press Speed Selector Button 2 for 15 seconds or until well blended.

3. In a mixing bowl, toss together all salad ingredients then top with vinaigrette and serve.

TIP — Vinaigrette can be kept in an airtight container in the refrigerator for up to one week.

★★★★★
PEANUT BUTTER
DREAM STACK

MAKES 6 STACKS

INGREDIENTS

1 cup heavy cream

1/4 cup store-bought peanut butter powder

2 tablespoons powdered sugar

30 chocolate wafers

Raspberries for garnish (optional)

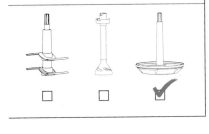

METHOD

1. Place heavy cream, peanut butter powder and sugar into the Chopper Bowl fitted with the Emulsifying Disc.
2. Press Speed Selector Button 1 for 15 seconds.
3. To assemble stacks, top one wafer with 1 tablespoon peanut butter mixture then top with wafer and repeat using 5 wafers for each stack.
4. Top each stack with 1 teaspoon peanut butter mixture then garnish with raspberries if desired and serve.

★★★★★ CINNAMON FROTH

MAKES 1 1/2 CUPS

INGREDIENTS

3/4 cup skim milk
2 tablespoons powdered sugar
1/2 teaspoon ground cinnamon

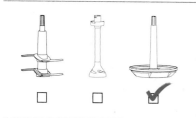

METHOD

1. Place all ingredients into the Chopper Bowl fitted with the Emulsifying Disc.

2. Press Speed Selector Button 1 for 12 seconds or until frothy.

3. Use this flavored froth for topping your hot tea or coffee.

TIP
Add pumpkin pie spice or nutmeg during the holidays.

ORANGE CUMIN VINAIGRETTE

★ ★ ★ ★ ★

MAKES 1 CUP

INGREDIENTS

For the Vinaigrette:

1 1/2 teaspoons Dijon mustard

1 teaspoon ground cumin

1/4 teaspoon crushed red
pepper flakes

1 1/2 teaspoons orange zest

1 tablespoon freshly squeezed
orange juice

1/4 teaspoon kosher salt

1/4 teaspoon black pepper

1/4 cup rice vinegar

2/3 cup grapeseed oil

For the Salad:

2 cups baby spinach

1 hard boiled egg, sliced

1/4 cup cherry tomatoes, halved

1/2 cucumber, sliced

1/4 shallot, thinly sliced

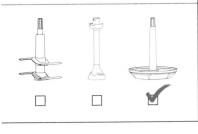

METHOD

1. Place all vinaigrette ingredients into the Chopper Bowl fitted with the Emulsifying Disc.

2. Press Speed Selector Button 2 for 15 seconds or until well blended.

3. In a salad bowl, toss together all salad ingredients then top with vinaigrette and serve.

TIP

Vinaigrette can be kept in an airtight container in the refrigerator for up to 1 week.

107

Simple Maple Whipped Cream

= MAKES 1 1/2 CUPS =

INGREDIENTS

1 cup heavy cream
1/4 cup real maple syrup

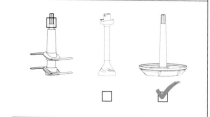

METHOD

1. Place all ingredients into the Chopper Bowl fitted with the Emulsifying Disc.
2. Press Speed Selector Button 1 for 15 seconds or until creamy.
3. Use as desired on coffee, hot tea or your favorite pie.

POMEGRANATE VINAIGRETTE

★★★★★

MAKES 1 CUP

INGREDIENTS

For the Vinaigrette:

1/2 cup pomegranate juice

1/4 cup red wine vinegar

1/2 cup grapeseed oil

2 tablespoons honey

1/4 teaspoon kosher salt

1/4 teaspoon black pepper

1/2 teaspoon chives, finely chopped

For the Salad:

4 cups baby spinach

1 cup mozzarella cheese, shredded

1/2 cup carrots, shredded

1/2 cup fresh raspberries

METHOD

1. Place all vinaigrette ingredients into the Chopper Bowl fitted with the Emulsifying Disc.
2. Press Speed Selector Button 2 for 15 seconds or until well blended.
3. In a salad bowl, toss together all salad ingredients then top with vinaigrette and serve.

TIP — Vinaigrette can be kept in an airtight container in the refrigerator for up to 1 week.

★★★★★ QUICK CHOCOLATE MOUSSE

MAKES 1 1/2 CUPS

INGREDIENTS

1 cup heavy cream
1/4 cup chocolate syrup
Shaved chocolate for garnish
1 Maraschino cherry for garnish

METHOD

1. Place heavy cream and chocolate syrup into the Chopper Bowl fitted with the Emulsifying Disc.
2. Press Speed Selector Button 1 for 15 seconds or until creamy.
3. Serve topped with shaved chocolate and a cherry.

TIP — For a lighter treat, use sugar-free chocolate syrup.

INDEX

INDEX